Theatre Ad Infinitum

BUCKET LIST

Theatre Ad Infinitum
Written by Nir Paldi
Devised with the company

T0347908

Bucket List was first performed at Pleasance Theatre Edinburgh on 3 August 2016 with the following cast:

Milagros Vicky Araico Casas

Norma/Teresa/Bertita/The Prawn /Miranda 44/Interviewer/Doctor Charlotte Dubery

Magda/Josue/Vasilij Stefanie Sourial

Maria/Jenny/Annabelle Deborah Pugh

Vere/Joe/Aunt Orian Michaeli

Singer/Presidents of the USA/Mexican President/Silva/Officer Dominguez/Mayor Fontañes/CEO of Connfox Amy Nostbakken

Live musician Haruna Komatsu

The touring production of *Bucket List* opened at Battersea Arts Centre on 13 February 2017 with the following cast:

Milagros Tamsin Clarke

Norma/Teresa/Bertita/The Prawn /Miranda 44/Interviewer/Doctor Charlotte Dubery

Magda/Josue/Vasilij Luisa Guerreiro

Maria/Jenny/Annabelle Deborah Pugh

Vere/Joe/Aunt Orian Michaeli

Singer/Presidents of the USA/Mexican President/Silva/Officer Dominguez/Mayor Fontañes/CEO of Connfox Shamira Turner

Live musician Haruna Komatsu

Writer/Director Nir Paldi

Designer Max Johns

Light Designer Peter Harrison

Sound Designer Chris Bartholomew

Musical Director/Composer Amy Nostbakken

Movement Director/Dramaturg George Mann

Producer Rosie Scudder for Battersea Arts Centre

Stage Manager Lauren J Cameron

Press Representative Mobius Industries
emma@mobiusindustries.com
Integrated BSL interpreter Jo Ross

Bucket List was inspired by an idea from Vicky Araico Casas

TOUR SCHEDULE

7 Mar	Bristol Grammar School
10–11 Mar	Heads Up Festival, Hull
14–16 Mar	The North Wall, Oxford
17–18 Mar	Platform 8 Festival, Peterborough
21–22 Mar	Chats Palace Arts Centre, London
23 Mar	Gosforth Civic Theatre, Newcastle
24–25 Mar	Jabberwocky Market Festival, Darlington
29–30 Mar	Tolmen Centre, Cornwall
31 Mar–1 Apr	Strike a Light Festival, Gloucester
4–5 Apr	Brewhouse Arts Centre, Burton
8 Apr	Doorstep Theatre Festival, Torbay
11 Apr	Guildhall Arts Centre, Grantham
12 Apr	Lincoln Drill Hall
13 Apr	Nottingham Lakeside Arts
14–15 Apr	Wigan Arts Festival
18–20 Apr	Birmingham Repertory Theatre
21 Apr	Paint the Town Festival, Medway
24 Apr	The Space, Sevenoaks School Performing Arts Centre
25 Apr	The Marlowe Theatre, Canterbury
26–27 Apr	The Lowry, Salford Quays
28–29 Apr	Looping the Loop Festival, Thanet

Tour supported by Battersea Arts Centre

Bucket List was created thanks to the generous support of Arts Council England, Battersea Arts Centre, Bristol Old Vic, The Lowry, The North Wall, Redbridge Drama Centre, Theatre in The Mill, Salisbury Playhouse and Anglo Arts.

CAST

Charlotte Dubery

Charlotte Dubery is a theatre-maker, performer and puppeteer. Charlotte studied Drama at the University of Exeter, and trained at École Jacques Lecoq in Paris. Driven by her passion for visual storytelling and creating theatre as an ensemble, she has performed, written and directed theatre for indoor and outdoor shows across the UK and internationally. Recent collaborations include; *Bucket List* (Theatre Ad Infinitum); *Light* (Theatre Ad Infinitum); *Golem* (1927); *Soul Song* (Lucy Catherine, Hive House Films) and *Paris Pieds Nus* (Abel et Gordon, Courage Mon Amour Films).

Deborah Pugh

Deborah Pugh is a theatre-maker and movement director, originally trained at École Internationale de Théâtre Jacques Lecoq. She is a core member of Theatre Ad Infinitum, developing and performing original work with them since 2007. Work with the company includes *Bucket List, Light, Ballad of the Burning Star* and *Translunar Paradise*.

As a movement director recent credits include *The Twits* (Curve Leicester); *Spitfire* (Lowry Theatre); *Declaration* (Lowry Theatre); *Bassett* (Sheffield Crucible); *Thesmophoriazusae* (Theatre In The Mill); *Lost Carnival* (Victoria Park, Crewe); *Kristin Lavransdatter* (North Wall) and *Breakin' Convention* (Sadler's Wells).

Deborah is also a visiting practitioner at a number of drama schools and universities. In 2017 she will be celebrating 10 years working with Ad Infinitum.

Haruna Komatsu

Haruna Komatsu is a clarinettist, taiko drummer, songwriter and multi-instrumentalist from Japan. Her own band "NO CARS" consists of three Japanese girls and a raccoon and has a reputation for transcendent quirkiness. She lives in London.

Luisa Guerreiro

Luisa Guerreiro trained at The Royal Central School of Speech and Drama, and Royal Holloway, University of London.

Luisa is a physical comedy actress with Cirque du Soleil, a professional puppeteer, performance capture and voice-over artist, musical theatre performer, movement artist/ choreographer and a highly proficient advanced stage and screen combatant. She is a fearless actress, physically and emotionally, in any medium of performance she undertakes. Credits include work with CBBC, BBC3 Comedy, Pinewood Studios, Centroid Studios, Audiomotion Studios, National Theatre, Young Vic, Sheffield Crucible, York Theatre Royal and Ragdoll Productions.

Orian Michaeli

Orian Michaeli is an Israeli choreographer, dancer and actress working in Israel and around the world. Her education includes the Visual Theater School in Jerusalem and the Ga'aton School for Dance. She has worked with choreographers Smadar Yearon, Ido Tadmor, Merav Cohen, Idit Herman, Iris Marko, Michal Herman, and Root Siglis. With directors: Nir Paldi, Moni Yosef, Osnat Shnek Yosef, Haled Abu Ali, Yeara Perach.

Orian choreographed *Mouthpiece* (Quote Unquote Collective); *This Might Hurt A Bit* (Max Stafford Clark – Out Of Joint); *Pitcairn* (Max Stafford Clark – Out Of Joint); *Ballad of the Burning Star* (Nir Paldi – Theatre Ad Infinitum); *Quite, The Tired Hero* (Avi Gibson – Acco Theatre); *Talented Like a Demon* and *To the Past*.

Choreography and acting in films include *Goose Bumps* (Director: Hadas Noiman) which won the Friendly Crowd Award in the Southern Cinema Festival, *It's Not All That Simple* (Director: Hadas Noiman) and *Fairy on the Roof* (Director: Hadas Noiman) which won the First Prize Award at the Apus Festival Tel-Aviv. Orian was the recipient of the Keren Sharet Foundation Scolarship and the Lohamei Hagetaot Museum Award. Currently creating a choreography for Quote Unquote Collective's new work *Now You See Her*. Orian is also a pilates and dance instructor.

Shamira Turner

Shamira Turner is an actor, musician and theatre-maker based in London. She is a founding member of award-winning Little Bulb Theatre, and has co-devised and performed in *Orpheus* (Battersea Arts Centre, Royal Opera House Linbury Studio, Salzburg Festival); *Operation Greenfield* (Soho Theatre, UK Tour); *Crocosmia* (BAC, UK & International Tour); *The Marvellous and Unlikely Fete of Little Upper Downing* (Tobacco Factory, UK Rural Tour); *Sporadical* (Forest Fringe, Shunt Vaults); *Goose Party* (Summerhall, Mayfest) and *Squally Showers* (National Theatre Shed) which have garnered Fringe First, Arches Brick, Total Theatre and Herald Angel awards. Shamira is co-director of emerging company She Goat, and performs in *DoppelDanger*. Additional theatre includes Robert in 1927's *Golem* (Young Vic; Trafalgar Studios; International Tour); actor/musician in Compagnie L'Immédiat's *La Machinajouer* (Salle de La Galerie in Fuveau); *Le Cabaret Calamiteux* (La Brèche in Cherbourg). Television credits include performer/accordionist in *CBeebies The Nutcracker* (BBC, 2016).

Shamira trained at the University of Kent, including a year at the University of California in San Diego, and on courses at RADA and the New York Film Academy. *Bucket List* is Shamira's first collaboration with Theatre Ad Infinitum.

Tamsin Clarke

Tamsin Clarke studied at Ecole Internacional Jacques Lecoq in Paris.

Since leaving she has written, directed and performed two shows under her theatre company, Popelei Theatre. *Knowledge of Angels* was a stage adaptation of the Booker-nominated novel by Jill Paton Walsh staged at St Leonard's Church in London. *Manuelita* premiered at the Edinburgh Festival in 2014 and won a Three Weeks Editors' Award ('Top 10 Shows of the Fringe') and critical acclaim ('a wonderful, warm performance that will have you leaving on a high' *The Stage*, ****). *Manuelita* will be touring Latin America in 2017 in both Spanish and English. Outside of Popelei, she has worked as a performer and deviser in the UK and abroad; DreamThinkSpeak's *In The Beginning Was The End* (2013) and PopUp Theatrics' *Long Distance Affair* (2014).

CREATIVE TEAM

Director/Writer Nir Paldi

Nir Paldi is a writer, director, performer and co-artistic director of Theatre Ad Infinitum.

He directed and co-adapted the company's *Odyssey*. *Odyssey* won the Stage Award, The Small Scene Theatre Festival Award in Croatia and was nominated for a Total Theatre Award. *Odyssey* has toured the globe since its première in 2009 and in 2015 Nir directed a one-woman Norwegian language version of *Odyssey*. Nir co-wrote and directed *The Big Smoke*, a critically acclaimed piece that won an Argos Angel Award, Nir's second Award for Best International Show at the United Solo Festival 2014 in New York City, and was nominated for a Canadian Dora Award and a Manchester Theatre Award. Nir wrote, directed and performs in *Ballad of the Burning Star*. *Ballad* won Nir his second Stage Award, and an OffWestEnd Award for its London run at Battersea Arts Centre in 2014. Nir directed and wrote Ad Infinitum's latest piece, *Bucket List*, which premiered at the 2016 Edinburgh Festival Fringe to critical acclaim and won the 2016 Spirit of the Fringe Award.

As an international freelance director, Nir co-wrote and directed *Juana in a Million*, which won him a Scotsman Fringe First Award and The United Solo Festival Award in New York City. Nir co-wrote and directed *Game of You* in Sao Paulo, Brazil, which was performed in April 2013. In Mexico, Nir directed and co-wrote *Milagros*, commissioned by Vicky Araico Casas which is currently touring.

Designer Max Johns

Max Johns trained in theatre design at Bristol Old Vic Theatre School. In 2015 he was awarded a BBC performing arts fellowship with Bristol Old Vic during which time he designed *Life Raft*, *Medusa* and *The Light Burns Blue*.

Other recent productions include *Kes* (West Yorkshire Playhouse); *Hamlet* and *All's Well That Ends Well* (Shakespeare at the Tobacco Factory); *Twelfth Night* (The Orange Tree); *Bucket List* (Theatre Ad Infinitum); *There Shall Be Fireworks*

(The Plasticine Men); *Under a Cardboard Sea* (Bristol Old Vic); *The Merry Owls* (The V&A Museum); *Strawberry & Chocolate* (Tobacco Factory Theatres); *Infinity Pool* and *DOGTAG* (Theatre West); *A Christmas Carol* (The Old Red Lion); *An Elephant in the Garden* (Poonamallee Productions); *London Road, Dutchman* and *The Merry Wives of Windsor* (BOVTS) and *Enron, The Eleventh Hour* and *Our Town* (The Egg).

Lighting Designer Peter Harrison

Peter Harrison trained at RADA.

His recent Lighting Designs include *Britten in Brooklyn* (Wiltons Music Hall); *Pink Mist* (Bristol Old Vic, Bush Theatre); *In Nocentes*, and *Home Turf* (Sadlers Wells); *Bucket List* (Theatre Ad Infinitum); *Alfie White: Space Explorer* (Tall Stories); *Run* (Vault Festival); *Marsha – A Girl Who Does Bad Things* (Arcola Theatre) and *The Twentieth Century Way* (Jermyn Street Theatre).

Other lighting design credits include *Much do About Nothing* (Ludlow Festival); *The Ballad of the Burning Star,* and *Translunar Paradise* (also for Theatre Ad Infinitum); *Jerry's Girls* (St. James Theatre); *Orestes* (Shared Experience); *The Doubtful Guest* (Hoipolloi); *Wuthering Heights* (Tamasha Theatre Company); *Once We Were Mothers* (Orange Tree, Richmond) and numerous pantomimes for First Family and Evolution Productions.

His opera credits include *Paul Bunyan* (Welsh National Youth Opera); *Orpheus in the Underworld* (Royal College of Music); *Carmen* (Hampstead Garden Opera) and as an Associate, *Written on Skin* (Festival d'Aix en Provence).

Other work as an Associate Lighting Designer includes *Collaborators*, and *As You Like It* (National Theatre); *Made in Dagenham* (Adelphi Theatre); *I Can't Sing* (Palladium) and *The Commitments* (Palace Theatre, London).

Sound Designer Chris Bartholomew

Chris Bartholomew is a composer and sound designer based in South London. He has worked extensively with devising and physical theatre companies including Theatre Ad Infinitum (*Light*, *Bucket List*); Curious Directive (*After the Rainfall*) and Idle Motion (*Shooting with Light*, *Voyager*). As a composer, Chris's work blends the acoustic and electronic. He has been commissioned by the London Acapella Festival, Portsmouth Festivities and the London Mozart Players, to create works for concert hall, cathedral and helipad.

Musical Director/Composer Amy Nostbakken

Amy Nostbakken is Co-Artistic Director of Quote Unquote Collective, a multi-disciplinary performance company based in Toronto, Canada. An award-winning playwright, performer and musician, Amy is a graduate of École Internationale de Théatre Jacques Lecoq in Paris.

She has created numerous award-winning productions including the one-woman show, which she co-wrote, composed and performs – Theatre Ad Infinitum's *The Big Smoke* (Edinburgh Fringe 2011). *The Big Smoke* was the winner of an Argus Angel Award and the award for Best International Show at the Solo United Festival in New York City 2015. As a member of Theatre Ad Infinitum Amy has also performed in *Ballad of the Burning Star* and *Bucket List* for which she also acted as musical director. Amy directed, co-wrote, composed and performs the multi-award winning *Mouthpiece*, which premiered in Toronto in 2015. *Mouthpiece* received six Dora Mavor Moore Award nominations, was awarded two and has toured Canada including Alberta, Manitoba, British Columbia, the Yukon and across Ontario. Currently Amy is developing Quote Unquote Collective's *Now You See Her* – an all female Rock opera. Amy teaches theatre and voice and runs Master Classes for industry professionals.

Movement Director / Dramaturg George Mann

George Mann founded Theatre Ad Infinitum in 2007, writing, directing and performing in the critically acclaimed, *Behind the Mirror* at Blue Elephant Theatre, London 2007 and at Edinburgh's Festival Fringe 2008. George co-devised, co-wrote and has continued to perform *Odyssey* around the world since 2009. He received The Stage Best Solo Performer Award for the adaptation of Homer's classic co-written and directed by Nir Paldi. He wrote, directed and performs in *Translunar Paradise*, which premiered at the Edinburgh Festival 2011-12, has won nine awards and toured all over the UK and the world. In 2014 He wrote, directed and performs live vocals in *Light*, which premiered in London at Barbican as part of the 2015 London International Mime Festival, before touring the UK. It has had two more London runs at Battersea Arts Centre and toured China in Oct-Nov 2016. George co-directed and co-devised the Christmas show, *Town Hall Cherubs*, a collaboration for 18-month to five-year-old children at Battersea Arts Centre for Dec 2015-Jan 2016, a critically acclaimed production nominated for two OffWestEnd Awards.

George won the National Theatre and Bristol Old Vic's Quercus Trust Award in December 2014 and became Associate Director at Bristol Old Vic. Credits include associate director for *The Crucible* directed by Tom Morris and movement director for *Sleeping Beauty* directed by Sally Cookson. In 2015 he co-directed Owen Sheer's dramatic poem, *Pink Mist*, a critically acclaimed production, which transferred to Bush Theatre, London in 2016 and toured the UK in 2017.

Stage Manager Lauren J Cameron

Lauren Cameron is a freelance stage manager and theatre designer. She graduated from the Technical Theatre course at ALRA in 2012, and has worked in different capacities with a wide variety of theatre companies since. She has been working with Theatre Ad Infinitum for three years and is proud to have facilitated the creation of *Bucket List* from the show's initial development stage.

Theatre Ad Infinitum is a multi-award-winning international ensemble based in Bristol that develops new and original theatre for multi-cultural audiences. We all share a passion for innovative theatre making that speaks to a global community, and create performances that harness the universal language of the body. Drawing on our differences in culture, nationality, and language we produce a unique and engaging form of theatre unified by our commitment to the audience.

That you may be moved, challenged and inspired by our work is our first priority.

Productions include *Bucket List* (2016); *Town Hall Cherubs* (2015-16); *Light* (2014); *Ballad of the Burning Star* (2013); *Translunar Paradise* (2011); *The Big Smoke* (2010); *Odyssey* (2009) and *Behind the Mirror* (2008).

www.theatreadinfinitum.co.uk
@TheatreAdInf

BUCKET LIST

BUCKET LIST

Theatre Ad Infinitum
Written by Nir Paldi
Devised with the company

OBERON BOOKS
LONDON

First published in 2017 by Oberon Books Ltd
521 Caledonian Road, London N7 9RH
Tel: +44 (0) 20 7607 3637 / Fax: +44 (0) 20 7607 3629
e-mail: info@oberonbooks.com
www.oberonbooks.com

A catalogue record for this book is available from the British
Library.

PB ISBN: 9781786821294
E ISBN: 9781786821300

Cover: Photograph by Alex Brenner
       Design by extra Strong

Characters

MILAGROS (Sometimes referred to as 'Mila')

SINGER

MARIA

VERE

JENNY

MAGDA

TERESA

JOSUE

BERTITA

ANNABELLE

VASILIJ

DOMINGUEZ

CEO

MAYOR

POTUS (President of the United States)

MEX. PRES (Mexican President)

SILVA

DOCTOR

NORMA

MIRANDA 44

THE PRAWN

INTERVIEWER

JOE

PR

PART ONE

The stage is bare. Throughout the play, all objects are mimed. Interaction between movement, text, light and music creates spaces and atmospheres. Performers play multiple characters switching from one to the other seamlessly. The actor playing MILAGROS doesn't change. There's a curtain made of strips of transparent plastic hanging all across the back of the stage. Behind it hang five coat hangers. The script is to be performed by five female actors and one female actor/singer. Live musician to one side of the stage.

Actors come in and form the shape of a bed. MILAGROS steps out of the bed.

MILAGROS: Sometimes it's hard to know what is real and what's not.

ANNOUNCEMENT: Ladies and Gentlemen, President Bill Clinton.

Through the curtain enters President Bill Clinton. The KIDS run in all different directions and disappear in the corners of the stage.

POTUS: In a few moments, I will sign three agreements, which will conclude our negotiations with Mexico and Canada to create NAFTA, The North American Free Trade Agreement. NAFTA means jobs. American jobs. Good-paying American jobs.

Now, for the last 20 years in all the wealthy countries of the world, the middle class has been under severe stress. Most Americans are working harder for less. The only way we can recover the fortunes of the middle class, the only way we can pass on the American Dream of the last 40 years to our children and their children for the next 40 years is to adapt to the changes which are occurring.

Now, most Americans don't know this, but the average Mexican citizen – even though wages are much lower in Mexico, the average Mexican citizen is now spending $450 per person per year on American products. Now, that is more than the average Japanese, the average German, the average Canadian or British buys.

So when people say that this trade agreement is just about moving jobs to Mexico, how do they explain the fact that more Mexicans are buying more American products every year? Mexican citizens with lower incomes spend more money – real dollars, not percentages of their income – more money on American products than the average British, Germans, Japanese, Canadian. That is a fact. And there will be more if they have more money to spend. That is what expanding trade is all about.

1. HIDE AND SEEK

As soon as Clinton finishes his speech, KIDS run from stage corners to play the game. MILAGROS narrates intermediately stepping out of the action and back in to it.

BERTITA: 1...2...3...4...5...6...

MILAGROS: I was born on the day this speech was given. The day NAFTA was signed.

BERTITA: 7...8...9...10

MILAGROS: 11 years later, in an industrial town in Northern Mexico we were living with the consequences.

MILAGROS and VERE hide in a box – JOSUE is left outside.

BERTITA: *(Turning around seeing JOSUE crouched and hiding behind his hands.)* Ayyyyy no Josue, you're supposed to hide! Josue? *(He's not responding just keeps hiding behind his hand.)* Josue come on!

JOSUE: But I was hiding!

BERTITA: You weren't hiding! You're so stupid!

JOSUE: I'm not stupid. You are stupid.

MILAGROS: *(MILAGROS pops out of the box in which she was hiding with VERE.)* We used to play outside all the time. I loved all the kids in the neighbourhood. But my favourite one, was my cousin; Vere. *(She gets back into the box.)*

SINGER sings as MILAGROS whispers into VERE's ear.

SINGER: *(Singing.)* I will throw a little stone and then they'll look the other way, and we'll capture the flag.

There's a noise. The cast react, and run across the stage. MARIA enters.

2. THE LIST

MARIA: Milagros!

MILAGROS: I lived with my Mom in a little hut made of old American garage doors.

MARIA: Mila!!!

MILAGROS: I have to go!

VERE: Why?!

MILAGROS: My Mom is calling me…

MARIA and MILAGROS cross the stage spin around one another changing the space to the hut where they live.

MARIA: Milagros! I told you a hundred times, you have to stay close to the house! You were too far away Mila. It is dangerous!

MILAGROS: You used to let me play wherever I wanted, why is it dangerous now?… Mom?

MARIA walks USC to a Chessboard to continue a game they've been playing.

MARIA: Come, let's carry on this game… Come on, it's your move…

MILAGROS goes to the Chessboard, she looks at it.

MILAGROS: Mom, you moved the pieces!

MARIA: Excuse me??

MILAGROS: My queen wasn't there?! And my knight was on this square?

MARIA: Well, at the very most I moved your queen, but I did not touch your knight...

MILAGROS: Mom!!!

MARIA: No! Of course I didn't move your pieces, come on..., it's your move!

MILAGROS: Mom, why is it dangerous now?... *(MARIA doesn't reply.)*

MARIA: Come on...it's your move...

MILAGROS: Mom?...

MARIA takes a letter out of her pocket and gives it to MILAGROS.

MARIA: I didn't want to tell you, but it's important, you need to know what's going on. Here, read it...

MILAGROS takes the letter, looks at it and reads out loud.

MILAGROS: 'To the bitch Maria. If you keep protesting you will die'. *(She looks up at her mother very scared.)*

MARIA: *(She looks at MILAGROS, brave and reassuring.)* Don't be scared. That is exactly what they want. We just have to be careful alright?

MILAGROS: But, Mom, what will you do?

MARIA: Well, I will keep protesting, until they meet with me and they explain to me why they think that this is okay! Have a look on the back. I've written all the names of all the people responsible for what is going on here.

MILAGROS: Number one. Señor Silva...your factory manager?

MARIA: Exactly! One of us! The Dog! For him, every woman is a bone – if you knew what he does to your Aunt Teresa everyday in his office. And these foreign bosses are like his masters, he'll obey anything they tell him to do…like opening the pipelines whenever it rains. They think we don't know that they are flooding our streets with poison and destroying our river. Every second family in this neighbourhood has lost someone to cancer. Your chest pain Mila? It's him!

MILAGROS: Him?

MARIA: Yes, him! I'm sure this prick Silva would love to put a bullet in my brain, but he doesn't have the balls. He'll have to pay someone to do it for him, just like the CEO pays him.

MILAGROS: The CEO? He is number two.

MARIA: Yes, Señor Puentes of Connfox, with his big stupid glasses. He pays the third on the list, Mayor Fontañes, to look the other way as he continues poisoning our streets. Do you remember what he promised us when he got elected? He said he would make all of this stop. But he is more interested in money, Mila. Money and his moustache! They are both clowns.

MILAGROS: 4. The Mexican President, 5. The American President… *(MARIA reads this with MILA.)*

MARIA: These two upholding the NAFTA agreement which takes away all our rights…

MILAGROS: I know, you told me –

MARIA: You need to hear it again! This agreement is between three countries: U.S.A., Canada and Mexico. Do you think that it brought so much pollution to the other two? No! Just Mexico! Do you think that in Canada there are millions of people working for 12 hours with no breaks? No! Just in Mexico! Because our President allows it. He isn't protecting our rights. You know, in Mexico worker's rights aren't bad, but in this NAFTA agreement they signed them away –

they turn a blind eye if the factory is under the agreement. It's always the weak ones that suffer. We suffer so that they gain. It has been like that for centuries.

MILAGROS: But Mom…what can we do?

MARIA: The first thing is to keep protesting, we cannot give up.

MILAGROS: But, how will you meet them –

MARIA: Shhhhh…we need to sleep now,

MILAGROS: Mom – tell me!

MARIA: Come on, I need to be at work soon.

Cast move to make diagonal bed USL MILAGROS and MARIA get into it. MILAGROS steps out.

MILAGROS: Following the NAFTA agreement, all along the border with the US, a lot of western companies opened Maquiladoras, assembling factories like Samsung, American Airlines, Gap, BMW, Honeywell, Hyundai, Sony, Sanyo, Samsonite, Canon, Casio, Fisher-Price, Ford, JVC, General Motors, Toshiba, Tiffany, Phillips, Daiahu, Nissan, Motorola, IBM, Coca-Cola, McDonalds and more and more and more. People, people from all over Mexico, came to our little town in search for the jobs that suddenly emerged. My mother, she worked in one of these Maquiladoras, and every day, she would wake up at 4 in the morning, so that she could be there on time.

Guitar begins lead into a song about MARIA's morning routine.

SINGER: *Maria…wakes up, and boils an egg for Milagros.*
Maria…changes into her factory uniform.
Maria…walks for an hour, to the bus in the dark. You know, women go missing and are murdered here everyday, so Maria… will run the whole way.

3. MAQUILA #1

Space change into the Maquiladora. The women are working each one in her station and talking to one another.

MILAGROS: My Mom and her friends worked for a large manufacturer called Connfox that makes electronic parts used in Blackberrys, iPads, iPhones, iPods, Kindles, Playstations, Xboxes and Nokias. They were getting paid, 39 cents an hour. If they are late even one minute – they're fired. They have no protection from the chemicals and can't go to the toilet during the shift so they get bladder pain. They stop drinking water, which stops the bladder pain, but then they get crazy headaches.

MARIA: Things are going to change you will see! I've got journalists coming to cover the demonstration. They will stop dumping this poison on our streets if it's the last thing I do!

TERESA: We're all behind you Maria; you're doing the right thing.

MILAGROS: Teresa, before working in this factory, she worked for Unilever – putting caps on deodorants;

MAGDA: Maria, I think you are being stupid and careless! You have a child to take care of.

MILAGROS: Auntie Magda, she had the longest Maquiladora career. She used to work for American Airlines constructing the screens for the chair backs in planes. Before that she worked for Nestlé sealing milk powder bags and before that, she was assembling TV flyback transformers for Sanyo.

MAGDA: Maria, what if they make good of their death threat? –

This is interrupted by the appearance of the factory manager Señor Silva, who gestures for TERESA to come with him to his office. The women stop talking and pretend to be very concentrated on their repetitive jobs until Silva and TERESA leave through the curtain.

TERESA takes her jacket off. Space changes. We see the women washing cloths together. We see TERESA completely broken and helpless due to the continuous harassment by Silva The Dog.

4. WASHING CLOTHES

TERESA: *(Running out from curtain and putting her jacket back on.)* I can't take it anymore…

MAGDA: Teresa! I told you the last time he did this; leave the factory! He won't stop. I've seen it happen so many times.

TERESA: I can't just leave the factory. I have to eat! It's not fair. There must be something I can do.

MARIA: You need to give him a reason to get his hands off you!

TERESA: What do you mean?

MARIA: Speak to the journalist who's covering the demonstration. I have her number. Let's ring at the end of the shift. We can expose him.

TERESA: No Maria, I don't want that.

MARIA: I know it is difficult, but you need to think about all the women you'll be helping. He has to be stopped.

TERESA: I can't Maria, I'm not as brave as you. I think I should go to the police.

MADGA/MARIA: The police?!

MARIA: You'd be better off doing nothing.

MAGDA: This is going to end up very badly. If the policemen don't rape you themselves, they'll go to The Dog and he'll take care of you.

TERESA: You don't understand, Magda. The cocaine, it makes him so violent. I have to make him stop –

MAGDA: Listen to me; going to the police is a big mistake Teresa.

5. DECLARO LA GERRA #1

MILAGROS: *(MILAGROS bursts from the scene.)* Teresa didn't listen – that evening, she went to the police.

Space changes to outdoors. KIDS are playing. ANNABELLE is about to step on JOSUE's foot and win the game. They all cheer.

JOSUE: Noooo – don't step on me!!!

ANNABELLE does and she wins!

ANNABELLE: I'm Brazil!

JOSUE: I'm Canada!

MILAGROS and **BERTITA:** I'm Mexico!

VERE: China!

MILAGROS: *(To BERTITA.)* NO!

BERTITA: *(To MILAGROS.)* England?

MILAGROS: Yes.

ANNABELLE: I declare the war against my worst enemy who is…!

JOSUE: Ay! *(To MILAGROS.)* Put your foot down…

MILAGROS: Bertita was the same –

BERTITA: Milagros didn't have her foot down either!

ANNABELLE: Everybody has to put your foot down!

MILAGROS: We need a rule!

ALL: *(Groans of annoyance.)*

MILAGROS: Okay, if any of us, lift, a, foot, we get a slap… *(To each of the children.)* agreed? Agreed? Agreed?… Vere! *(Goes up to her and threatens her.)* Agreed?

VERE: *(Thinking and then quietly.)* Yea.

15

ANNABELLE: I declare the war on my worst enemy who is…
Mexico!

*The KIDS run to the corners for MILAGROS to choose whom she's
going to attack.*

MILAGROS: Stop! I declare war on Vere – I'm going to kill
you with one elephant step! One…

*VERE moves her foot just before MILAGROS stamps on it – she broke
the rules.*

MILAGROS: *(Annoyed.)* VERE! You lifted your foot! Oh, now I
will have to slap you!

*MILAGROS spits on her hands preparing them for the slap and the
rest of the KIDS run to intercept VERE as she tries to escape, dragging
her up to USR.*

KIDS: She lifted her foot! Oooohhh! She broke the rule!

VERE: What! You can't hit me for real! Leave me alone! Leave
me alone!

MILAGROS: But it's the rules! I have to hit you!

VERE: Let me go! I'm going home. I'm not going to play with
you anymore. You are my worst enemy!

MILAGROS: No, you are my worst enemy –

JOSUE: Ahhhhhhhh!!!!!! *(Pointing USC, screams with terror.)*

BERTITA: What is it?!

JOSUE: It's a head! It's a head!

MILAGROS: What is it?! *(They run over.)*

BERTITA: It's a head! It's a head!

JOSUE: Don't touch it! Don't touch it!!!

MILAGROS: Shut up Josue!

MILAGROS walks DS and narrates, the rest follow her.

MILAGROS: Teresa's eyes were open. Her hair was wet, like she'd just got out of the shower. On the skin of her neck you could see the pattern left by the knife that hacked her head from her body. Her body parts; arms, legs, torso were lying there like a butchered pig. I felt a pain in my chest.

Space changes to MARIA's hut. It's MARIA and MILAGROS now.

6. THE NIGHT BEFORE THE DEMONSTRATION

MARIA: He will pay for this! You will see Mila. He will pay for this.

MILAGROS: Mom... I don't want you to go to the demonstration tomorrow.

MARIA: I know.

MILAGROS: Please don't go. Please don't do it...

MARIA: I have no choice. We have no choice.

MILAGROS gets a very strong pain in the chest.

MARIA: Shhh... Are you okay Mila? *(MARIA comforts her.)* Tomorrow after the demonstration we're taking you back to the Dr. He lied, this is not an allergy.

MILAGROS: I'm fine Mom – it comes and goes.

MARIA: Everyone needs to know what is going on here. The World needs to know that we are being poisoned, that we are being slaughtered like animals!

As MARIA gets more and more into a speech the space transforms from her hut to a demonstration.

7. MARIA'S DEATH

Drum beat and space changes to demonstration.

CROWD: Hey Fontañes, You have blood on your hands! Hey Fontañes, You have blood on your hands! Hey!

MILAGROS: We were in front of the town hall. Hundreds of people were there.

MARIA: I have, in my hand, a letter warning me, no, threatening me, to stop these protests. But did I cower in fear? No! Their threats cannot stop us! So what did I do? I took this letter and on the back I wrote the names of the people responsible for our situation! We will not stop protesting and we will keep marching on the homes and offices of The Factory Manager, The CEO of Connfox, the Mayor, the Mexican President, the President of the United States of Americ –

MARIA is shot in the head and falls off to the floor. MILAGROS is very still. She's slowly moving towards her mother's dead body as she speaks.

MILAGROS: Everything stopped. I stood there, looking at what was left of my mother's face. My chest was very painful. I felt like I couldn't breathe. I went to her, I hugged her and then I felt it *(MILAGROS helps MARIA to stand up)*, the list covered with her blood. I picked it up and read the names. I passed out.

MILAGROS is pulled into the hospital bed.

PART TWO

8. MAGDA'S HUT

MADGA wakes MILAGROS up in the hospital bed.

MAGDA: Mila, Mila, Mila.

MILAGROS: Mom?!

Space changes, we're at MAGDA's hut.

MAGDA: Mila, it's Magda.

MILAGROS: I was living with Magda now. After my Mom's funeral I got into bed and didn't get up for 3 days.

MAGDA: I don't care if you are hungry or not child, if you won't eat now I will give you a smack.

MILAGROS: Magda wasn't young. She was harsh and set in her ways. She had no kids of her own, but my Mom was a bit like a daughter for her.

MAGDA: Look, what happened is very bad. Chicita, very, very bad. But your mother was a fighter and I'm sure she wouldn't have wanted you moping in bed all day – you've got to fight – you have to make a life for yourself. Okay Chicita?

MILAGROS: So I ate, I started to go out again – going to school, playing with my friends and then, after 2 years, in the summer when I was 13, I met Jenny McAdams.

KIDS are playing.

9. DECLARO LA GERRA #2

BERTITA: I declare the war on my worst enemy who is... United States!

JENNY: *(Laughing.)* Hi there little guy! –

JOSUE: You are so beautiful!!!

SINGER: *(Sings as jazz drums kick in. The scene freezes every time the song-narration comes in.)* Jenny McAdams, 30-years-old, from Boston, Massachusetts...

JENNY: Me llamo Jennifer!

JOSUE: Jennifer! Ah, mama you are SO sexy!!

JENNY: I'm here from a charitable –

KIDS react by imitating JENNY. They mock her.

SINGER: *(Singing.)* She's got a life long fascination with Mexicoooooo.

JENNY: Organisation...

SINGER: *(Singing.)* She regrets, getting a tattoo of a dolphin on her lower back that she got during her spring break in Cancun.

KIDS surround JENNY.

JENNY: We are opening a community centre, un centro communitario for you guys...

BERTITA: Have you got any chocolate? *(Everyone laughs.)*...

SINGER: *(Singing.)* She's writing, a PhD Thesis, entitled 'Methods to prevent criminality in youth and promote excellence through the game of Chess in Industrial Towns of Mexico'.

JENNY: Chocolates? Ohhh you like chocolate – maybe I might have one. Maybe tengo solo uno chocolate, one. Okay, I have ONE chocolate bar! Compartir...share! –

BERTITA grabs the chocolate and runs away.

BERTITA: It's for Mila!!

BERTITA gives MILAGROS the chocolate. KIDS squabble over chocolate, MILAGROS gives some to VERE and they start to play Declarro again.

JENNY: So, the community centre will be open 5 days a week. We got sporting activities we got internet access, I will be teaching Chess. We open next Tuesday. Any of you guys know what Chess is?

MILAGROS: I know. I used to play with my Mom.

JENNY: Well alright then. So I hope to see you there on Tuesday.

VERE: Brazil!

Space changes – KIDS are gone and JENNY is by herself on the phone in the community centre.

JENNY: No, I'm fine – I had a little cry, but now I'm totally over it. Yea the kids are pretty wild, but I guess that's to be expected.

Me? No, I'm excited. I can't believe we finally open the centre today. I worked really hard to reach out to these kids.

Of course I'm nervous Jackass, I mean – what if nobody turns up? You know but at the end of the day it's not about me, it's about them. And…

Actually, yeah… There was one that could be right. She played a little Chess with her mom. Well, before her mom got shot… I dunno, like 13,14… Yea Toto, we're not in Kansas anymore.

KIDS are entering the community centre.

MILAGROS: Hey!

JENNY: Hey! You came! –

VERE runs in, steals JENNY's phone and starts talking into it. Group run around the space throwing it to each other. JENNY tries to stop them.

JENNY: *(Getting annoyed now – she feels she has to get control over the situation.)* HEY! HEY! HEEEEEEEEEEY! Okay…

We play, por la telephone, if you win you get the phone
if I win – it's mine!

MILAGROS: Ah we play for the telephone? Si Si! *(To the kids in Spanish.)* Ah, jugamos para el teléfono!!

KIDS list their countries, and gesture to JENNY to say one.

JENNY: Venezuela! Err… Declaro la guerra *(Pronounces wrong.)*

BERTITA: Guerra, Jennifer!

JOSUE: Guerra!

JENNY: Ah, okay. Declaro la guerrrrrrra with Mexico!

MILAGROS: Stop! I declare the war against Jennifer! And I'm going to kill you with 1 Frog Step.

KIDS: 1 step?????

MILAGROS: I mean – 2 frog steps –

JENNY: No you said 1 step Mexico, let's go!

MILAGROS: Okay, 1 frog step, 1… *(She doesn't reach JENNY – she loses.)*

KIDS react with anger and frustration. JENNY reaches her arm out asking MILAGROS for the phone after she won. MILAGROS hands it over.

JENNY: Now, my friends, I am looking for a great Chess player that will come with me in 6 months time back to the US to play in a huge competition – have you ever been to the States?

JOSUE: I come with you? I come with you!

The group, apart from MILAGROS, bursts into laughter. MILAGROS is interested.

JENNY: Okay maybe we start with the basics… *(They all sit on the floor around a Chessboard and JENNY teaches them the game.)*

10. RAPE #1

Space changes to the bed. MILAGROS can't sleep.

MILAGROS: Vere… Vere, are you asleep?

VERE: What?

MILAGROS whispers in VERE's ear, singer sings.

SINGER: *(Singing.)* Vere, I've got something to tell you- you're my worst enemy.

MAGDA: Shhh!

MILAGROS giggles, then whispers.

SINGER: *(Singing.)* Is that right Mila? Is that right? Well, what are you going to do to me?

Laughing, whispering. Mock fighting full of affection.

MAGDA: Shhhh!

SINGER: *(Sings as MILAGROS.)* Let's get out of here!

VERE: Now?

SINGER: *(Sings as MILAGROS.)* I'm hot! Let's get out of here!

VERE: No!

Fantasy escape sequence – shown in dance. Then suddenly SR. DOMINGUEZ grabs VERE…

DOMINGUEZ: Woah, what do we have here?

MILAGROS approaches him and tries to grab VERE so they can leave.

DOMINGUEZ: *(To MILAGROS.)* Hey, whoa what the fuck do you think you're doing, huh? Did I tell you you could move? You stay right here little girl. *(Pushes MILAGROS.)* And you, go home.

Pushes VERE USL as chorus start humming.

DOMINGUEZ: Is this your first time inside of a cop car?

Movement sequence during song. The women represent the rapist as VERE trys to escape them.

SINGER: *Look in my eyes*
　　　　Don't have to cry
　　　　Be a good girl
　　　　And you won't die
　　　　Lay down
　　　　Lay down
　　　　Lay down
　　　　Surrender

MILAGROS runs SC to find VERE lying on the floor.

MILAGROS: Vere, Vere… Vamos a casa… *(To audience.)* That was the first time I met Officer Dominguez. He developed a taste for Vere.

Vere, are you okay?

VERE is completely shocked by the experience.

We are going to tell Tia Magda. We will go to the police.

VERE: We will not tell anybody.

MILAGROS: Vere we have to do something! He has to PAY!

VERE: No!!

MILAGROS: We have to talk to Tia Madga, she'll help you –

VERE: NO!! WE ARE NOT GOING TO TELL ANYBODY.

MILAGROS: We have to do something!

VERE: We will not tell anybody, WE WILL NOT TELL ANYBODY, WE WILL NOT TELL ANYBODY!

They hug as VERE becomes upset and cries.

MILAGROS: Okay, okay, okay…

Space changes – KIDS playing.

11. WHERE IS THE GIRL?

MILAGROS: Okay, okay, okay… Okay so you are a shitty man that took a girl out of her home and you killed her and you cut her into pieces and you hid her in the desert so no one would find her, but I'm going to get this information out of you Josue! You understand me?

JOSUE: *(He's playing the part.)* Of course.

The KIDS are acting out her directions.

MILAGROS: Okay! I'm gonna come up to your face and look right up in to your face and look into your eyes and ask: where is the girl Señor? *(JOSUE starts pointing out at VERE.)* You don't answer! I say it louder: Where is the fucking girl?!

ANNABELLE: What do I do?

MILAGROS: Annabelle, grab him by the wrists and pull his arms back strong so it hurts him. Now you, you can say you don't know, but then I'll slap you in the face because you're lying. Or you spit into my face, and then we hammer a nail into your knee. Then you tell me where the girl is, tell me where the girl is –

JOSUE runs downstage to VERE, grabbing a hold of her.

JOSUE: She's here! Come on Vere! *(Mimes having sex with VERE.)*

MILAGROS: Que pasa?! Dejala?!

MILAGROS grabs JOSUE, pushing him to the ground – pulls him slaps him hard. The group rushes to JOSUE's side and MILAGROS stands there alone. A pause.

MILAGROS: I'm sorry.

Space changes into the community centre.

12. CHESS LEARNING MONTAGE

They move into the community centre, they are playing at the Chessboard.
KIDS apart from MILAGROS are not paying attention. JOSUE is trying
to interrupt and distract MILAGROS.

JENNY: *(To MILAGROS.)* Your play is too emotional; you got
to use your head more. Take control of that centre early.
Think tactically at all times. Okay, have a look where that
bishop is right now... You got options you see – we can
play it safe, we can bring him across here.

MILAGROS: Not safe...

JENNY: Okay in that case, lets see what happens if you bring
it down here. First thing that's gonna happen is that my
knight is going to think it's her birthday because if you
move the bishop here.

JOSUE stands behind JENNY and starts pretending that he's
masturbating. The girls laugh. MILAGROS notices him first and
then JENNY.

JENNY: Guys, there are rules!

MILAGROS: Josue, what the fuck! *(MILAGROS pushes JOSUE they*
push one another.)

JOSUE: Why, you want some?

MILAGROS: No, I don't! Stop it!

JOSUE: Come on, Milagros!

MILAGROS: Stop it I said!

JOSUE: Cinga tu madre pendaja!

MILAGROS: Cinga la tua!

JOSUE: A la cingada. *(He walks off.)*

MILAGROS goes back to sit by JENNY.

MILAGROS: Continue Jenny.

JENNY: Okay.

SINGER: *(Singing.)* The king takes one step up or down,

The rook goes as far as she desires.

JOSUE: Let's go Vere!

VERE: Milagros, are you coming?

MILAGROS: Jenny, can I come back tomorrow?

JENNY: Sure you can!! I'll be here from 10 to 6 so just come whenever you like.

The group move up and around in a circle to the next day as we see MILAGROS and JENNY meet again and again to make progress on her Chess.

SINGER: *The bishop moves diagonal,*
And the knight curves in an L,
As the pawn pushes on for the queen,
Who's there to protect her man,
Left or right, up and down,
Until he reaches his fate, in Checkmate.

MILAGROS: Hey!

JENNY: Hey, you came back!

They move into the factory layout around JENNY and MILAGROS, drums come in.

JENNY: Hola señorita!

MILAGROS: Hi Jenny! Her you?

JENNY: How are you?

MILAGROS: How are you!

JENNY: I am great, thank you. Shall we?

JENNY: Today, I want to teach you how to pin your enemy down. I'm gonna teach you a move called The Skewer. You ready?

MILAGROS: Yes!

Chorus move into a line diagonally across the space.

JENNY: The Skewer is an attack on two pieces in a line. One behind the other.

Chorus move as JENNY directs them as if they were the Chess pieces.

JENNY: To save the valuable piece, your opponent is gonna move it out the way – this exposes another, less valuable piece – which can then be captured.

Chorus fall down apart from MILAGROS.

MILAGROS: I got it...one piece behind the other, The Skewer!

Space changes into the hospital bed.

13. RAPE #2

MILAGROS: Vere, Vere, are you awake?

VERE: Mila, you need to rest...

MILAGROS: I can't –

VERE: Mila go to sleep.

MILAGROS: I can't stop thinking about the US!

MAGDA: Shush!

Hospital beep fades out. MILAGROS and VERE in bed.

VERE: Do you think you'll win?

MILAGROS: Yes!

VERE is laughing with joy at the dream MILAGROS just described.

VERE: I think you will go to the US and never come back.

MILAGROS: NO Vere!! I will never leave you here alone. One day, we will go to the US together. I promise you!

MILAGROS whispers in VERE's ear, SINGER sings:

SINGER: *One day, I promise you we'll have a big house with a pool,*
    And a big screen TV in every room, (Group starts salsa.)
    We'll eat steak dinners every day,
    And I'll buy a real fast car to drive us far away.
    So, let's get out of here!
    Let's get out of here!
    Come on, let's get out!

VERE and MILAGROS go dancing outside like before. SR. DOMINGUEZ grabs VERE. A series of images of the group as a combination of the women taking care of VERE and representing SR. DOMINGUEZ raping her.

    Look in my eyes
    Don't have to cry
    Be a good girl
    And you won't die

It ends with MILAGROS unable to sleep. Clarinet starts playing sleeping music, and cast moves into sleeping positions on floor CS. MILAGROS can't sleep and gets up. VERE isn't there. She gets out of the hut to look for her. She can't see her coming so she enters back to the hut and wakes MAGDA up.

14. THE SKEWER

MILAGROS: Auntie Magda, Auntie Magda!

MAGDA: What?

MILAGROS: Vere isn't here yet.

MAGDA: Mila, Mila we cannot do anything –

MILAGROS: We have to do something, can't you speak to a journalist? It has to stop!

MAGDA: Shush! Milagros don't you understand? This man is a police officer – if we speak to a journalist they'll be dead the next day, and so will Vere.

MILAGROS: But this has been going on for weeks –

MAGDA: I've seen this happen so many times. I'm begging you Milagros, you have to be patient. He will get tired of her and it will stop. Mila, look at me, you are such a smart girl – so smart! Please, use your brain!

MILAGROS: I am using my brain, I want to help my friend!

MAGDA: Don't you remember what happened to your mom?

MILAGROS: I do! They killed her and then the protests stopped! They got exactly what they wanted.

MAGDA scoffs and goes to bed in anger.

MILAGROS: As Magda left and got back into her bed, I made a decision – I wasn't going to keep my head down. I wasn't going to let this bastard get away with it! I started following Vere and Dominguez.

VERE runs and gets into bed. We see DOMINGUEZ and VERE and MILAGROS is part of the image following them.

I found out exactly where he was taking her each night. I followed the blue light on his car. I got to know his habits, his routine. Lowering her seat. Getting on top of her. I could see his naked back through the windshield. Completely engrossed in what he is doing to her. The doors are always unlocked. I had a plan for Dominguez… One piece behind the other. The Skewer.

Sequence finishes with VERE exhausted laying in bed. Sharp change into new space.

15. LA BRITNEY

KIDS are playing Britney.

MILAGROS: Okay. We're gonna stand in a square and I'll be number 1 as La Britney. Number 2, number 3 number 4 number 5. Number 2 back left, number 3 back right, 4 and 5 in the middle. When I push to the front, you all move along with me as my backup. Number 2 and number 3 two steps to the left. Number 4 and number 5 two steps to the right. If you forget or you fuck up…you do the snake.

Beat then heavy breaths x4 as group stands in 'snake position'.
SINGER sings as the group dances in the square formation:

SINGER: *Baby, don't you wanna, dance up on me,*
    To another time and place,
    Baby don't you wanna, dance up on me,
    Leaving behind my name and age…
    I'm a slave for you… (Repeats x3.)

The image of the KIDS dancing transforms into a Maquila image.
We see VERE and MILAGROS standing and working.

16. KILLING DOMINGUEZ

MILAGROS: Vere and I were 14. We were working at the Maquila. I was ready. Dominguez was going to pay. Tonight. Vere! Come!

MILAGROS reaches her hand to VERE and they start salsa dancing together. They spin and VERE moves away USL when DOMINGUEZ comes DSC. DOMINGUEZ stands behind VERE as before.

MILAGROS: I had a knife in my hand. I knew exactly what I was going to do. In the dark I hid by the side of the car. He was on top of her for the last time. I opened the passenger door and then – *(MILAGROS mimes stabbing DOMINGUEZ in the back repeatedly.)*

Aztec Death Whistle sound. VERE walks towards MILAGROS. They hug. MILAGROS holds her by the shoulders and says;

MILAGROS: Vere this is over now. You must never talk about this to anyone. You understand me? *(VERE gestures yes.)* I have water and clean clothes with me, we can change on the way home. Lets get out of here.

They run away and MILAGROS gets a very strong pain in her chest.

17. CANCER DIAGNOSIS

MILAGROS is in great pain she almost can't talk. She steps out of the situation and speaks to the audience.

MILAGROS: I've been getting this pain in my chest since I was very young. But it has never been this bad. Vere helped me to get home. She called Jenny and they took me to the hospital. After a long wait I was seen and tested.

MAGDA, JENNY and VERE are in the hospital with MILAGROS.

DOCTOR: Milagros? There is no easy way of saying this. I've looked at your scan, and you have cancer. The tumour is very aggressive and it has already spread to many of your vital organs – you must have been in pain for a long time.

We see the chorus creating a short montage of the traumatic moments in her life – her mother is shot.

MILAGROS: My Mom took me to see a Doctor at her Maquiladora when the pain started but the Doctor said it was just an allergy.

DOCTOR: They always say that, but it is them. It's the chemicals from their factories. It's in the air, it's in the water, it's on the workers clothes when they come home each night and hug their children. *(DOCTOR fades out.)*

MILAGROS is at the front full with shock and rage. We see the chorus continuing the short montage of moments in her life – VERE is raped, stabbing DOMINGUEZ and then Maquila movement, running – her emotional state grows more and more intense as she stands CS. At the end of the montage we flash back to the DOCTOR.

DOCTOR: I'm very sorry but there's nothing we can do, other than keep you here and make you comfortable, but this is very expensive so I'd advise you go home…

JENNY: No, no, no, she's covered by the charity's insurance *(JENNY moves DSL, taking off her demin jacket and becoming MARIA.)* I can arrange all the funding, I just need you to make sure that she is as comfortable as possible –

JENNY stands DSL and is shot in the head as MARIA.

DOCTOR: Okay, I'll prescribe her some strong painkillers, but these might cause hallucinations. We don't know for sure but in our care, she can have anything between a week and a few months –

MILAGROS is pulled back into the bed by the chorus, but she fights against it, escaping. They all take their blue jackets off slowly and sink to the ground. MILAGROS stands and throws her jacket to the ground after taking it off.

MILAGROS: Sometimes it's hard to know what's real and what's not. As I heard the words coming out of the Doctor's mouth, I couldn't stop thinking about my mother's list.

MILAGROS stands DSC and starts her monologue – guitar kicks in again.

I gave them all animal names – Silva, The Dog *(the cast pant x3)* was the easiest to get to. He lived in the better part of town with his wife and their 3 little children. The Mayor, *(the cast stamp x3)* I called him The Rabbit, he had 19 children; he owned a football team, a racetrack and a giant casino in the middle of the city. The CEO of Connfox, *(the cast look back and forth over their shoulders).* The Fox, lived in San Diego but visited Mexico for business meetings and special events. The Mexican President, *(the cast raise arms and hiss).* The Snake lives in Mexico city, with his latest wife who's an actress and their 6 children, all from previous marriages. The American President, *(the cast raise arms in slow flaps x2).* The Eagle, lived in Washington, in the White House, just like his daddy, with his wife and their twin girls. He used to be an alcoholic before he found God. I kept researching more and more but had no clue how will I ever get to them, especially the Presidents. I didn't have much time. I had to act now.

PART THREE

Space changes, MILAGROS is playing Chess with JENNY.

18. MILAGROS ASKS JENNY TO TAKE HER TO US

MILAGROS: Checkmate!

JENNY: You are getting better by the day my friend!

MILAGROS: Jenny, I have to go to this competition. Really Jenny. It's so important for me. It can change everything!

JENNY: I agree. You worked really hard. You deserve it.

MILAGROS: What do I have to do?

JENNY: Nothing. You leave it with me; I'll speak to the committee.

Space changes to the Maquiladora.

19. 1, 2, 3

MILAGROS is speaking to us as she's working. She's thinking about ways of killing Silva. The above is interrupted by scenes with JENNY at the Chess club.

MILAGROS: I had Jenny working on getting me to the US, that was a start. I had to move fast on the rest of the list. Number One: Silva, he arrives at the factory at 8 a.m. sharp every day. I can kill him at the factory or follow him and kill him on his way home. Or kill him in his home. No, this would be too difficult. He has a family.

Space changes to Chess club we see MILAGROS and JENNY.

MILAGROS: Jenny, what did they say?

JENNY: Mila it might take a couple of weeks. Listen, you need to be prepared that it might be a no. Okay?

MILAGROS: No. No. They have to take me.

Space changes back to Maquiladora.

MILAGROS: I have to get him here at the factory. Fuck! Cameras! This factory is completely covered with cameras. How do I do it? There must be a way!

Space changes to Chess club.

MILAGROS: Jenny, did they say anything?

JENNY: Mila! What is going on? Look I promise you, the second they make a decision I will let you know.

Space changes into Maquiladora. The chorus is working while MILAGROS is narrating DS.

MILAGROS: Weeks past and I didn't make any progress. I didn't have any news from Jenny and every idea I came up with about The Dog seemed more stupid than the other.

Space changes to Chess club. They are mid-game.

JENNY: This is a mistake! You had a classic decoy just in front of your eyes. You move your bishop here, then you have my queen pinned down to my king and my queen will have to capture your bishop but then you get me. Look! You got me! A perfect decoy.

MILAGROS: I got it!

Space changes back to Maquila.

Finally! I noticed a pattern.

We see Silva taking one of the women – behind the curtain similarly to what he did with TERESA earlier.

Everyday, at 11 a.m., Silva takes a worker called Norma into his office – just like he used to do with Teresa. He's obsessed with this Norma. I need to use her to get to him. But I didn't know Norma. I'd never spoken to her. I had to find a way.

As NORMA bursts through the curtain, space changes to a lockers area where employees get changed at the end of their shift at the

Maquiladora. We see NORMA opening her locker and MILAGROS hiding and peeping behind a corner to see the locker number. As NORMA turns to her locker:

MILAGROS: Locker 567. Locker 567. That's where I can find her.

Space changes back to Maquila working. Silva takes NORMA behind the curtain again.

MILAGROS: I'll pay her to be 'sick' and miss work one day. And then when Silva comes looking for her I will step up and say 'Señor Silva, Norma isn't here today and she asked me to tell you personally'... NOOOOO! This is stupid! If he'd be dead when I leave the room everyone will know I did it!!! Think Milagros think! It needs to be simple. Clean. I was watching her everyday. She will be my decoy.

Space changes to a lockers area. We see MILAGROS approaching NORMA who is crying.

MILAGROS: She looked sad and lonely. She often cried. She needed someone to talk to.

MILAGROS: *(Touching NORMA's shoulder.)* Are you okay?

NORMA: I'm fine.

MILAGROS: I just saw you crying and I thought...

NORMA: I can't take it anymore!!!

MILAGROS: What is it?

NORMA: I can't talk about it.

MILAGROS: I understand. If you need any help...

NORMA: Look I really can't talk about it.

(Pause.) MILAGROS takes a risk and addresses the issue directly.

MILAGROS: He used to do the same to my Aunt Teresa.

NORMA: Teresa was your aunt?

MILAGROS: Yes.

NORMA: I'm sorry. The Dog. He always threatens me that if I speak against him I'll end up like Teresa.

MILAGROS: Bastard! You have to be careful.

NORMA: You don't understand. The cocaine makes him crazy – I sometimes wonder how I'm still alive!

MILAGROS: *(To audience.)* The cocaine! I'll poison his cocaine! With rat poison! It wouldn't be me; it would be the cocaine that was off… He'll be found dead somewhere like a dog.

NORMA: And the worst thing is that I have to get it for him everyday! He doesn't even have the balls to get it himself.

MILAGROS: Wait, you buy it for him?!

NORMA: No! His men leave a bag in my locker. Anyway, I need to get home to my children. What's your name?

MILAGROS: Milagros.

NORMA: I'm Norma. Milagros please, please don't talk about this to anyone. He's a dangerous man and we can both end up like your aunt.

MILAGROS: Of course.

NORMA closes and locks her locker, while MILAGROS watches and memorises the code.

MILAGROS: D2611. Locker 567.

NORMA: Thank you.

MILAGROS: *(To audience.)* I'll replace the bag and she will deliver the poison.

Space change. JENNY walking up and down the Chess club waiting for MILAGROS to arrive.

JENNY: There you are!!! I've been waiting forever – I was about to lock up. Where were you?

MILAGROS: Jenny, what's going on?

JENNY: Nothing much…it's just that I heard from the committee.

MILAGROS: And?

JENNY: Well… They said…that you sound real nice and very talented…

MILAGROS: Jenny tell me!

JENNY: You're coming with me to the US!

MILAGROS: Aaaaaaaa!

JENNY: You get one month training with a Chess-grandmaster. At the end of which, if you are ready and only if, you get to compete. You got two weeks, we leave March 22nd. Your flights are all booked!

MILAGROS: March 22nd. Thank you so much Jenny, I'm so happy. Do you mind if I stay here a bit? I want to practise. I can lock-up when I leave.

JENNY: Sure.

MILAGROS: As soon as she left, I jumped on the computer. March 22nd. I had two weeks to kill the three of them. I had a plan for The Dog, now; I needed one for The Rabbit Mayor and one for The Fox CEO. I googled The Rabbit – The first thing that came up was a video of him –

MAYOR: This city means everything to me. It is my home. It is where I raised my 19 children. For the last 10 years that I've been Mayor we've made much progress. However, the one area that still needs our attention is the pollution, that is like a cancer at the heart of our community. The 22nd March is World Water Day. What an opportunity to clean our river! I'm personally working in association with the CEO of Connfox to bring the community together on this special occasion. Events will take place all over the city so please visit the city hall website at www dot –

MILAGROS: Next, the Connfox website. There was a video of The Fox –

CEO: We've been working hard in collaboration with the Mayor's office to clean the pollution of the river. Ahead of March 22nd and the World Water Day celebration, we are looking to get the community involved by telling us why now is the time to clean the river. So please email us your stories – at

MILAGROS is typing…

MILAGROS: My name is Milagros Cervantes and my mother died fighting to end the pollution in this city. She was shot in the head as she was protesting…

MILAGROS' words are cut by PR words.

PR: *(On the phone.)* Am I speaking to Milagros Cervantes?

MILAGROS: *(To audience.)* A few days later I got a call… *(On the phone.)* Yes.

PR: I'm calling from the 'Clean River – Better Life' project. We read your story and everyone here in the PR office absolutely loved it. We feel it'd be such a waste not to use your mom's story. It could inspire people – it could inspire change.

MILAGROS: Okay…

PR: As you probably know, on March 22nd there'll be plenty of events happening all over the city and I want to know if you'd be available for a photo shoot with the Mayor and the CEO of Connfox?

MILAGROS: Sure! When? Where?

PR: Great! We will be opening a new viewpoint above the river; the event itself takes place lunchtime March 22nd. However, I'm also gonna need you to attend the rehearsal on the 21st. We want to do the photograph on the new viewpoint and we want you to cut the ribbon! I'll send you the address and all the details. Okay?

MILAGROS: Yes.

PR: Ah, one last thing, you work at the Connfox Maquiladora right?

MILAGROS: Yes.

PR: Can you wear your uniform for the photo shoot? We'll have someone to sort your hair out.

Space changes to bus.

MILAGROS: I put the phone down, got on the bus and went straight to the river.

Space changes to the viewpoint on the riverbank.

MILAGROS: I used to come here with my Mom. We'd stand there and she'd tell me stories…

MARIA is a memory in MILAGROS' head. They hold hands.

MARIA: Milagros, don't get too close! When I was a child, this river was clean. We used to swim in it for hours…but now you can't even think of swimming in it. Don't forget what happened to Guadalupe's Aldo, when he fell in. He was only going to get his football. At first he was fine but later that evening he started to vomit. Guadalupe she took him to the hospital and there the Doctor said he had arsenic poisoning. Hours later, he was in a coma. 18 days later he was dead.

MARIA is shot dead, falls to the ground. MILAGROS jumps up to face audience CS.

MILAGROS: I wish I could push the two of them into the water and finish them off like that! But that wouldn't work. I needed something else. The new viewpoint was about a 100 meters to my left. It stuck out of the riverbank and floated midair above the water. It was supported from underneath by two wooden posts. The platform was surrounded by safety railings. I was in front of it. How? How will I get them into the water and get away with that? I can't just push them, people will see me. I stepped on it. *(The platform shakes under MILAGROS' weight.)* It was shaky. It wasn't built well.

20. MARCH 21ST

Space change. JENNY and MILAGROS are at the centre for the last time, playing Chess. MILAGROS' mind is distracted.

MILAGROS: *(To audience.)* It was March 21st, the day before I left for the US. I still had no idea how to get them both into the river without getting caught.

JENNY: Milagros, you are so distracted! You could have created a double attack. If you moved your knight across you'd have threatened my rook and my king at the same time – a double attack.

MILAGROS: *(To audience.)* I was distracted! That's it! A double attack!

JENNY: Do you remember we're flying tomorrow? Is everything ready?

MILAGROS: Yes.

JENNY: I'll pick you up at 6. A taxi will take us straight to the airport.

MILAGROS: See you tomorrow at 6. *(Space changes to bus. To audience.)* On my way out, I grabbed an emergency axe next to the fire escape and put it in my bag.

21. THE REHEARSAL

Space changes to the viewpoint where the PR is explaining to MILAGROS and the rest how things are going to go in the event the next day. There's a whole team of people.

PR: Thank you everyone for coming to the rehearsal. Now let's get it done as soon as possible so we can get on with our day, okay? So first of all we've got the Mayor who's going to speak first – how beautiful and clean everything is going to look blablabla. And then the CEO will speak – thank you to our lovely volunteers I'm sure it's going to look great blablabla. We're going to do a photograph here and then head over to the viewpoint. Milagros, Milagros?

MILAGROS: Here. *(Puts hand up.)*

PR: This is where you come in – You will go with them. And you cut the ribbon. All clear?

MILAGROS: Yes.

PR: Good. We do a photograph on the viewpoint and there'll probably be questions from the journalists about your mom… I hope that's okay… *(Doesn't wait for answer.)* Great! Thank you – you can go. The rest of you, I want this place sparkling clean before tomorrow. You hang the ribbon and then that's it, no one touches it until tomorrow.

MILAGROS: I was hiding behind an old Coca-Cola billboard. Watching them preparing the viewpoint for the ceremony in the morning. They finished and left. It was getting dark. I walked toward the viewpoint, crawled beneath the wooden structure and got myself all the way to the very edge of the riverbank. Looking up, I could see the platform as it suspended directly above the water. The two supporting posts were on either side of me. I grabbed the emergency axe out of my bag.

MILAGROS mimes hacking into the wooden post.

I hack it just enough for it to support itself for now, but as soon as any weight is put on it, it will collapse.

MILAGROS is pulled back into the hospital bed.

MILAGROS: D2611, Locker 567…

NURSE: Milagros, what are you talking about?

MILAGROS pulls back into her fantasy as space changes to bus on her way to the Maquiladora.

22. MARCH 22ND

MILAGROS: It was March 22nd. I was on my way to the factory. Today at 6 I'll meet Jenny and fly to the US. If I don't fuck it up, by the time I'm on the plane – The Dog,

The Rabbit and The Fox will be dead. In my pocket I had
a plastic bag with powdered rat poison. Everyday at 10 to
11 Silva's man puts a bag of cocaine in Norma's locker.
At 5 to 11, Norma picks up the bag ready to meet Silva at
11. I had to swap the bags before Norma arrived.

Space changes to locker room at the factory.

Locker 567. D2611. I was entering the code on Norma's
locker –

*We see MILAGROS collapsing with pain on the floor in front of the
locker and then she's pulled into the hospital bed.*

NURSE: Milagros, I need you to take your painkillers…

Back into the fantasy.

MILAGROS: …it hit me like a hammer. I was on the floor,
I couldn't move. She will be here in a minute. It has to be
done today.

NORMA arrives.

NORMA: Milagros are you okay?

*MILAGROS is in great pain. She's looking at NORMA barely able
to talk.*

MILAGROS: *(To audience.)* FUCK! Now what? I fucked it up.
(To NORMA.) I'm fine. I get this pain in my chest. I need to
take my painkillers.

*NORMA opens her locker. She takes the cocaine out and puts it in her
bag as MILAGROS is saying:*

MILAGROS: No no no no no! She took the bag of cocaine.
What do I do? What do I do??

NORMA: Can I help you somehow? I only have a minute.

Space changes to hospital bed.

NURSE: The nurse will be along soon, Milagros!

MILAGROS: She took the bag of cocaine, she took the bag! –

NURSE: Would you like some water?

MILAGROS: Yes!

Back into fantasy and the locker room with NORMA.

MILAGROS: I just need some water so I can take the painkillers.

NORMA: Sure! Can you keep an eye on my handbag?

MILAGROS: *(To the audience, laughing.)* She left the bag! With me! *(To NORMA.)* Sure!

NORMA leaves running to get the water.

MILAGROS: I swapped the cocaine for the poison as fast as I could.

NORMA comes in with the water and gives it to MILAGROS.

NORMA: Here. I have to go, he's waiting. I'm sorry I can't help you more.

MILAGROS: No, Norma, you helped me more than enough. Thank you.

NORMA leaves.

MILAGROS: She left with the poison in her bag. She didn't know it, but soon her life will change for the better.

Space changes to bus.

MILAGROS: I waited there until the painkillers started working. When I was able to stand up I went straight to the 'Clean River – Better Life' event, leaving the factory for the last time.

Space changes to the event by the river.

MAYOR: I love this river! –

MILAGROS: *(To the audience.)* Press were everywhere. Cameras flashing in all directions. The Mayor was speaking –

MAYOR: Water is life, and this river is at the heart of our city, the heart of my family.

MILAGROS: *(To the audience.)* Liar! My Mom told me how The Rabbit got richer and richer; bribed by The Fox to look the other way as he poisoned our river.

MAYOR: And now I'd like to invite the CEO of Connfox, who's been so supportive with this project to say a few words.

CEO: Thank you. We've built this viewpoint as a promise to you that one day this river will be clean again.

MILAGROS: When they were done lying through their teeth we started moving towards the viewpoint.

MAYOR: Shall we cut the ribbon?

Space changes to the viewpoint. Photos are taken as MILAGROS cuts the ribbon.

MAYOR: A photo of the three of us Milagros?

They pose and the photo is taken.

MILAGROS: Sure.

MAYOR: After you young lady.

MILAGROS: NO! No, Mayor, please, please after you!

MAYOR: Okay. After you Señor…

CEO: Thank you.

The MAYOR and the CEO get on the viewpoint. Music creates suspense and chorus that's been creating railings are looking with anticipation to see whether or not the structure collapses as the two get on it. Nothing happens.

MILAGROS: They were both on the viewpoint but it didn't collapse! Shit! It needed more weight! What do I do? They have to die!

CEO/MAYOR: Come on board Milagros. Don't be shy.

MILAGROS: *(MILAGROS gets on the viewpoint – it still doesn't collapse.)* I held on to a railing standing next to them. But still this thing didn't move.

PR: *(PR is taking a photo.)* Smile!! Milagros... Smile!

MILAGROS: There was nothing to smile about, my plan is not working...

PR: *(PR approaches the viewpoint.)* Now I want you between them...look, here!

PR gets on the viewpoint – viewpoint collapses. Chorus goes forward with MILAGROS.

MILAGROS: They fell into the river. I held onto a railing for my life. Someone pulled me up. It was chaos. The Rabbit looked dead with his body floating. The fall must have got him. The Fox was very much alive, throwing his arms from side to side – I watched as more and more of the poison he created splashed into his mouth. Tonight, he'll vomit, fall into a coma and die! *(Space changes to bus.)* As soon as I could get away from the paramedics and the media I left. I was meeting Jenny at 6 and Vere was coming to say goodbye. In my head I crossed The Rabbit and The Fox off the list. I was thinking about The Dog,

Space changes to MAGDA's hut. VERE is waiting and MILAGROS arrives.

VERE: Mila! Where were you? It's almost six o'clock. I hope you can make it to the airport.

MILAGROS: What do you mean?

VERE: All the roads are closed.

MILAGROS: Why?

VERE: The Dog! He is dead.

MILAGROS: *(To audience, miming a scream of triumph.)* What!? How?!

VERE: They say he overdosed on cocaine in his office. There is police everywhere.

JENNY arrives.

JENNY: Hey Milagros, are you ready?

SINGER: *I got you a passport, I bought you a ticket,*
We'll fly you to New York, you'll never believe it.
We'll go to LA, Chicago, the Mid-West...

BERTITA hugs her and then they spin US.

We'll travel the country,
You'll beat the very best.
You'll learn from the masters,
You'll play all the winners,
Defeat them at their own game.
So come on, let's get out of here!
Let's get out of here!

Guitar stops. VERE whispers into MILAGROS' ear.

SINGER: *(Singing.)* Thank you! Thank you!... Mila, thank you...

We hear a loud airplane sound.

23. THE U.S.A.

MILAGROS: Straight from the airport, Jenny took me to my apartment and then to see the sights; the Statue of Liberty, the Empire State Building, a boat along the Hudson River, to see 'Chicago' on Broadway, to the movies, museums, shopping, roller blading, to try a hot dog, a milkshake, some cotton candy – Fuck! I don't have a plan for The Eagle! And even if I do, I have nothing for The Snake! I didn't do it right!

MILAGROS is very frustrated. MARIA appears and calls MILAGROS to continue a game of Chess with her.

MARIA: Milagros, come on…lets finish this game. It's your move.

MILAGROS is moving toward the board reluctantly.

MARIA: Look! You can promote this pawn. You bring this pawn to my last rank and it can become a queen.
Your pawn can become your queen. You have this game.

MILAGROS processes her mother's advice and starts to understand that she can 'pawn promote' her plot. MARIA puts the jacket on and turns into JENNY. She then grabs JENNY and puts her in position like when she first told her she's going to the US – she throws her denim jacket at her – rewind noise.

MILAGROS: Jenny! What did they say?

JENNY: Well, They said you seemed real nice…

MILAGROS: Tell me!

JENNY: You are coming with me to the US…

MILAGROS: No! *(She pushes JENNY downstage – rewind sound.)*

JENNY: You are coming with me to the US and if you win the competition you get to play Chess with the Mexican President!

MILAGROS: No! *(Pushes JENNY away.)*

JENNY: You are coming with me to the US and if you win that competition you will get to play Chess with the Mexican and the American Presidents!

MILAGROS: That's it.

Space changes to a corridor in front of VASILIJ's office.

JENNY: The most important thing is that you are not intimidated. Now, he's very strict. You ready?

MILAGROS: Yes!

JENNY: Good girl.

Knock on door.

VASILIJ: What?

He walks out.

JENNY: Vasilij Vasilijevich – this is Milagros Cervantes!

MILAGROS goes to shake his hand but he doesn't lift his hand.

VASILIJ: The Mexican defence 1920! The Mexican champion, Taura plays the US champion Marshall – he wins in only 7 moves. You, will win in 6. *(To JENNY.)* You can go. *(To MILAGROS.)* You, follow me.

They walk upstage.

VASILIJ: Milagros – it means miracles, right?

MILAGROS: Yes.

VASILIJ: Well, miracles are certainly not going to help you on the board, that's for sure… You are going to play against the best players in one month so you better focus. You will be white. Show me your first move. *(She goes to move.)* Ah! And, surprise me.

MILAGROS: White knight to C2…

VASILIJ: Good – but, I said surprise me.

Throughout the coming scene the space changes back and forth from training with VASILIJ to MILAGROS researching murder methods online.

MILAGROS: I was playing with Vasilij all day everyday.

VASILIJ: Checkmate!

MILAGROS: And when I wasn't playing.

VASILIJ: Checkmate!

MILAGROS: I was online. "How to kill someone with just a touch"…

VASILIJ: It is all about choosing the right attack for the situation.

MILAGROS: 25 methods for killing with your bare hands:

1. THE TEMPLE – A vital spot. When struck with sufficient force, will cause death.

Black Queen to H4

VASILIJ: No!!!

MILAGROS: But –

VASILIJ: Again! Again!

MILAGROS: White Knight to… White Knight to C6 –

VASILIJ: Checkmate!

MILAGROS:

2. HOOK TO JAW – A powerful punch to the jaw will snap an enemy's neck.

Pawn G5

3. ADAM'S APPLE – Asphyxiation. Ahhhh No!! This won't work. I'm not a ninja… –

Queen G5

VASILIJ: It's been 2 weeks and you are making the same mistakes. Yes, you are thinking big – but all your pieces are exposed. Dominate the centre! Go!

MILAGROS: 'Poison that kills instantly…'

VASILIJ: Look! White Knight to –

MILAGROS: Phenol – when inhaled or swallowed causes irregular breathing, muscle weakness, tremors, loss of co-ordination, convulsions and finally respiratory arrest… Kills within 2-3 minutes.

VASILIJ: Checkmate!

MILAGROS: Cyanide – when inhaled or swallowed prevents blood from carrying oxygen to the cells, resulting in cardiac arrest within seconds.

VASILIJ: Checkmate! Don't look at the board, see it in your mind.

MILAGROS: 'Poison that's absorbed through the skin:'

Miranda44:

MIRANDA 44: Hi everyone, I need to kill a character namely by the wearing of a poisonous dress. I heard this is called Contact Poison. Does this really exist?

MILAGROS: Pawn G5

The_Prawn_Identity:

THE PRAWN: Hi Miranda 44, the Golden Poison Dart Frog is the closest thing you get to actual contact poison. The play sounds intriguing, good luck with it all –

VASILIJ: Milagros, we have only one week of practise left and I'm really uncertain you can do it. I would expect, after so much practise that you'd be able to find the solution for this problem.

MILAGROS: Golden Poison Dart Frog…considered one of the most toxic animals on Earth. A single specimen measuring five centimetres has enough poison to kill 10 grown men.

VASILIJ: Good!

MILAGROS: Indigenous Emberá people of Colombia have used this substance for centuries to tip their blowgun darts when hunting, hence the species' name.

VASILIJ: Good!

MILAGROS: Hello, is this Scales of Justice? Hi, I'm looking for a Golden Poison Dart Frog? Yes but I need the Golden one. You have it? Tomorrow at 11? I'll be there.

Space changes to exotic pet shop. Shopkeeper named JOE meets her there.

JOE: It's just there.

MILAGROS: Do you have the gloves and everything I need…

JOE: You don't need any gloves.

MILAGROS: But…the poison?

JOE: Ah… *(Laughs.)* You thought this is the poisonous one? No no no, you can just touch it, look *(he goes and grabs a frog)* see?

MILAGROS: *(Extremely disappointed.)* But it's called a poisonous frog.

JOE: Yes, but they get their poison from a mix of insects that they eat in the rain forest. In captivity, they stop being poisonous after 2 or 3 years and the ones that are born in captivity aren't poisonous at all.

MILAGROS: So you can't get a poisonous one? You don't sell them?

JOE: It's illegal to sell it with poison.

MILAGROS: Well, never mind… *(Goes to leave.)*

JOE: Wait, wait! I didn't say I don't sell them. I just said it's illegal to sell it. Come, come… Why do you need a poisonous one?

MILAGROS: To kill the Presidents of United States and Mexico.

JOE laughs very hard.

JOE: It's expensive you know…

MILAGROS: Well, do you sell it or not?

JOE: Come with me –

JOE takes MILAGROS out back.

JOE: Gloves, no gloves, you can't touch it… You touch it, then touch your face, your eyes, your nose, your mouth and that's it, you're dead. You keep it in this box. You feed it with this –

MILAGROS: Wait – how do I know it is really poisonous?

We see JOE miming the below as MILAGROS say it.

MILAGROS: He took a mouse by the tail and lowered it down into the box. It was dead in 2 seconds.

JOE: Happy now?

MILAGROS: I'm happy.
　　　　　Pawn G4,
　　　　　Check,
　　　　　Bishop G5,
　　　　　Knight to F3,
　　　　　CHECKMATE!

Music stops suddenly on 'checkmate'. VASILIJ laughs and walks downstage to shake MILAGROS' hand.

VASILIJ: Dyevushka. You are ready, to compete. I will be there with you tomorrow.

SINGER: Welcome to the 3rd Annual North American Youth Chess Championship here at the beautiful Lincoln Centre…

Space changes to the competition. A physical montage takes place recapping MILAGROS' life in combination with images of MILAGROS taking part in the Chess competition and repeating MARIA's death a few times. MILAGROS won the competition.

JENNY: Oh my god! Oh my god! I can't believe it! *(JENNY and MILAGROS hug.)*

Suddenly, JENNY breaks out of the hug and she is now MARIA.

MARIA: Milagros! What are you doing with my list Milagros?! This is not how we fight these people!

MILAGROS: Your way of fighting failed Mom. What am I supposed to do?! Wait until they shoot me in the head?!

MARIA: We are not animals like them Milagros, we do not murder!

MILAGROS: They murdered you, and they are murdering me…

MARIA is now gone. MILAGROS is standing with JENNY and an interviewer after her victory.

24. COLLAPSE

INTERVIEWER: I am here with Milagros Cervantes, the 15 year old Mexican Chess Champion who is just about to play not one but two Presidents.

MILAGROS: In my hand I had a box. Inside the box I had a Chess piece. A queen.

Completely covered with poison. I am going to stab them one by one.

INTERVIEWER: You must be so excited.

MILAGROS: I was in complete pain. My chest was on fire. NO! NO! No! I have to stay strong!

INTERVIEWER: Could you share a few thoughts about how you're feeling today?

MILAGROS: *(To interviewer.)* I feel very excited…

MILAGROS is dragged back into the hospital bed. She steps forward to speak to the audience.

25. NUMBER 4

MILAGROS: I was taken to hospital. I was diagnosed with Stage 4 Terminal Lung Cancer. Again. I was so close – stupid lungs, why now? Couldn't you have held on – I'm not done –

MILAGROS is pulled back into the hospital bed. JENNY enters the hospital room. MILAGROS is staring into space not noticing her presence.

JENNY: Milagros, Milagros.

MILAGROS: *(To audience.)* I was in a lot of pain. Jenny was by my side for three full days. I was being sent back to Mexico.

JENNY: I know you are in pain but there's someone here who wants to meet you.

MILAGROS: I didn't care. All I could think of was that I didn't kill The Snake and The Eagle.

The MEXICAN PRESIDENT enters the room.

MEX. PRES: Milagros… Hola Milagros. Como te sientes?

MILAGROS: *(To audience.)* The Snake! He was in my room. What do I do? I can't stab him now! I'll be arrested and I'll never get to The Eagle.

(To PRESIDENT.) Sr. Presidente, thank you so much for coming here.

MILAGROS is waking up – she can 'smell blood'.

(To audience.) What if he just touches it? Jenny, I had a little box with me on the day I collapsed, do you know where it is?

JENNY: Yea sure, it's just here in my bag. Here.

MILAGROS: Did you open it?

JENNY: No. Here – *(Gives the box to MILAGROS.)*

MILAGROS: Sr. Presidente, the day that I was going to play with you, I wanted to use this piece.

MEX. PRES: May I?

MILAGROS: Please!

The MEXICAN PRESIDENT takes the piece from the box. He inspects it.

MEX. PRES: Mmmmm. This is a beautiful piece! Did you make it?

MILAGROS: *(To audience.)* I bought it in Chinatown for one dollar. *(To PRESIDENT.)* Yes.

MEX. PRES: Milagros, your story is inspirational. I know what you've been through and look how far you have come. The whole of Mexico is behind you. When I get back I'll ask my PA to contact you first thing, so we can play that game. *(Passes the piece back.)* But, you hang on to this – for when you beat me. Now you must excuse me – I have to give a speech at the UN.

We see the MEXICAN PRESIDENT giving a speech pressing his hands to his mouth.

MEX. PRES: There's no doubt in my mind that NAFTA will continue to create jobs, and improve the lives of the Mexican people.

Chorus stand and shoot towards audience with poison dart.

MILAGROS: I watched him on CNN. Pressing his hands against his lips, like he was praying, to show how genuine he was. Sucking up my poison. Then in front of the whole world…he died.

Death whistle noise transforms into hut clarinet.

MILAGROS: The foam on his mouth looked just like the foam on the polluted river back home.

Space changes to MAGDA's hut.

MILAGROS: I flew back to Mexico. I laid in bed for two weeks. I was dying, I could feel it. I failed! I failed! Now I'd never get to him.

VERE: Mila, can I get you anything? I need to be in the factory in five minutes but Magda will be here soon.

MILAGROS: I'm fine.

Cellphone rings.

VERE: It's your phone. Here. *(Gives phone to MILAGROS.)*

MILAGROS: Hello?

JENNY: Milagros, it's Jenny.

MILAGROS: Hi Jenny.

JENNY: Milagros, I did something that I hope will make you very happy. Have you ever heard of a charity called 'Make A Wish'?

MILAGROS: No.

JENNY: They make wishes come true for young people with terminal illness. I wrote to them and told them your story and how you missed meeting the American President.

MILAGROS: *(To audience.)* Now she had my full attention.

We hear the sound of an airplane.

26. NUMBER 5

Space change to The Oval Office. JENNY helps MILAGROS walk in.

JENNY: WOW! Will you look at this place! I can't believe I am standing in The White House.

POTUS enters from USL. JENNY is still behind MILAGROS.

POTUS: Milagros! I'm so happy to meet you and I'm so pleased that you're here. I was really sorry when we couldn't play that game.

JENNY: I'll leave you to it.

POTUS: Ah no, Jenny! Jenny – I heard a lot about you too you know. People like you are exactly what America needs. Exactly what the world needs. Someone who's willing to travel to the corners of the world to give kids a chance.

If it wasn't for you I wouldn't be meeting this young lady... Milagros... Can I tell you something? You are an inspiration, to me, to my staff and most importantly to every single young girl who just needs a strong role model. Someone who's brave, someone who's a fighter, someone who never gives up. And that's you Milagros.

MILAGROS: Thank you so much for doing this Mr President.

POTUS: It's my pleasure.

MILAGROS: Playing you has always been my greatest wish.

POTUS: Shall we play?

MILAGROS: *(Smiles.)* Yes.

MILAGROS is nearly sucked into hospital bed but resists.

POTUS: I got to tell you, I played a few games of Chess back in my Yell days and wasn't that bad. However, I never, in my entire life, played a world champion such as yourself. Be easy on me alright?

MILAGROS: I can't make that promise, Mr President.

POTUS: Good answer! Now would you like to play white?

MILAGROS takes out the box with the queen in it, opens it and presents it to the President.

MILAGROS: Can I use my lucky queen?

POTUS: That's a beautiful piece you've got there.

We see MILAGROS taking out her queen piece of the little wooden box and offering it to POTUS – she mimes scratching POTUS with the piece.

POTUS: *(Shocked.)* Milagros!

MILAGROS: ...and then I scratched him with my Queen.

POTUS: What are you doing?

MILAGROS: I just killed you.

POTUS: What are you talking about?

MILAGROS: This Chess piece, this queen, is completely covered in poison – you'll be dead in three minutes…

POTUS: Why would you do this?

MILAGROS: You are at the top of a chain of people that are torturing us, raping us, poisoning us and using us so you can be comfortable. You have the power to change and you do nothing! –

MARIA steps forward DSR.

POTUS and **MARIA:** You think you can force change by killing me? The second I'm gone – there will be somebody else standing in my place. And now, you are a killer. You can kill me – but you can not kill a system!

MILAGROS: What am I supposed to do?! What am I supposed to do?! Tell me! Tell me, TELL ME! *(The questions are directed straight to the audience.)*

MILAGROS is pulled back as she repeats 'tell me' into hospital bed – she stops shouting and moves through the curtain. The cast form her family members around her hospital bed. Pause. The family members move back into doing their Maquiladora movements.

Beat then Blackout.